Chinese
Horoscopes

each element and thus the modifications they produce within each sign are:

Metal – fixity, strength of will, fluency of speech.
Water – powers of reflection, sensitivity, persuasiveness.
Wood – imagination, creativity, idealism, compassion.
Fire – dynamism, passion, energy, aggression, leadership.
Earth – stability, reliability, practicality, industry, prudence.

Applying the elements to the animal signs means that there will not only be subtle differences between, say, a Metal Rat and a Water Rat, but also that although the Rat sign itself may recur every 12 years, because its accompanying element varies over five successive cycles, it follows that the same elemental Rat will not repeat itself again for 60 years. In simple terms, the Metal Rat occurs in the first set of 12 years, the Water Rat in the next 12, the Wood Rat in the following 12, the Fire Rat next, and finally the Earth Rat in the last 12-year group – a sequence which in all lasts for 60 years.

At present we are in the cycle that began with the Wood Rat on 2 February 1984 and which ends with the Wood Pig on the 18 February 1996.

So, although as a group the twelve signs constitute a perpetually repeating cycle, given that the *complete* cycle actually runs for 60 years it is clear to see that the same influences will not exactly repeat themselves every 12 years, as it first appeared. Yet, of course, there will be fundamental similarities within the same sign recurring every 12 years and thus, as my teaching colleague recognised, albeit subconsciously, there will also be the same fundamental similarities between all subjects born within the same year.

It is, however, as plain as the nose on one's face that even within the same year class not every child will be merely a clone of the next, but that glaring differences between the individuals exist. And it is here that the complexities of the Chinese horoscope come into play.

Apart from categorising people into years, and modifying those years with the five elements, Chinese astrology further refines individual characteristics according to the negative and positive forces attached to each year, according to the month or season in which a person is born and, further still, according to the very hour in which that individual comes into the world.

Chinese wisdom sees a polarity in every element, a negative and a positive side, an essentially feminine (passive) or masculine (active) disposition or, in Chinese terminology, Yin and Yang. Consequently, each element is repeated twice in succession so that, taking the element Wood, for example, it presents in the first year its Yang, or masculine side (represented by +), and reverses the next year into its Yin polar opposite (represented by −). So this is why a teacher may find one year more passive, and by implication, less strenuous to teach than the following, livelier, more assertive, year's intake.

Further variations may be laid on top of the year sign, the element and the polarity by adding into the equation the month of birth which corresponds thus:

January	Rat
February	Ox
March	Tiger
April	Rabbit
May	Dragon
June	Snake
July	Horse
August	Sheep
September	Monkey
October	Rooster
November	Dog
December	Pig

And still further refinement of the character is made by calculating the very hour of birth and adding that, too, to the other layers of analysis. The Chinese divide their day into two-hourly periods, beginning at 11 pm and the signs, headed by the Rat, follow in their sequence each governing one of the two-hour periods in turn. Thus the day's rulership appears as:

11 pm –	12.59 am	Rat
1 am –	2.59 am	Ox
3 am –	4.59 am	Tiger
5 am –	6.59 am	Rabbit
7 am –	8.59 am	Dragon
9 am –	10.59 am	Snake
11 am –	12.59 pm	Horse
1 pm –	2.59 pm	Sheep
3 pm –	4.59 pm	Monkey
5 pm –	6.59 pm	Rooster
7 pm –	8.59 pm	Dog
9 pm –	10.59 pm	Pig

So, under the Chinese Astrological system a complete analysis of an individual would have to take into account: 1. Year of Birth, 2. Element, 3. Yin/Yang polarity, 4. Month of Birth, 5. Hour of Birth.

When analysing an individual, then, it is the year sign that lays down the fundamental description of character, but this character is subject to refinement by the element, polarity and animal characteristics governing both the month and hour of birth. Thus, each variation in turn adapts and modifies the behaviour and motivation of the individual, each layer of interpretation adds greater refinement, rather like an artist's sketch where each layer of paint is applied in turn, until the whole, unique picture that describes the personality is complete.

Indeed, it may be seen that Chinese astrology is a deep and complex subject when all the layers of analysis are overlaid. And yet, despite its complexity, it still allows ample scope for an individual to glean fascinating information about his or her personality even from a mere cursory glance at its ancient and compelling wisdom.

This chart, taken from the Chinese perpetual calendar, lays out each year for the whole of the 20th Century, and an additional short pace into the 21st, together with each year's animal sign, its element and its masculine and feminine principle.

YEAR CHART

YEAR	FROM – TO	ANIMAL SYMBOL	ELEMENT	ASPECT
1900	31 January 1900 – 18 February 1901	Rat	Metal	(+)
1901	19 February 1901 – 7 February 1902	Ox	Metal	(−)
1902	8 February 1902 – 28 January 1903	Tiger	Water	(+)
1903	29 January 1903 – 15 February 1904	Rabbit	Water	(−)
1904	16 February 1904 – 3 February 1905	Dragon	Wood	(+)
1905	4 February 1905 – 24 January 1906	Snake	Wood	(−)
1906	25 January 1906 – 12 February 1907	Horse	Fire	(+)
1907	13 February 1907 – 1 February 1908	Sheep	Fire	(−)
1908	2 February 1908 – 21 January 1909	Monkey	Earth	(+)
1909	22 January 1909 – 9 February 1910	Rooster	Earth	(−)
1910	10 February 1910 – 29 January 1911	Dog	Metal	(+)
1911	30 January 1911 – 17 February 1912	Pig	Metal	(−)
1912	18 February 1912 – 5 February 1913	Rat	Water	(+)
1913	6 February 1913 – 25 January 1914	Ox	Water	(−)
1914	26 January 1914 – 13 February 1915	Tiger	Wood	(+)
1915	14 February 1915 – 2 February 1916	Rabbit	Wood	(−)
1916	3 February 1916 – 22 January 1917	Dragon	Fire	(+)

YEAR	FROM – TO	ANIMAL SYMBOL	ELEMENT	ASPECT
1917	23 January 1917 – 10 February 1918	Snake	Fire	(−)
1918	11 February 1918 – 31 January 1919	Horse	Earth	(+)
1919	1 February 1919 – 19 February 1920	Sheep	Earth	(−)
1920	20 February 1920 – 7 February 1921	Monkey	Metal	(+)
1921	8 February 1921 – 27 January 1922	Rooster	Metal	(−)
1922	28 January 1922 – 15 February 1923	Dog	Water	(+)
1923	16 February 1923 – 4 February 1924	Pig	Water	(−)
1924	5 February 1924 – 24 January 1925	Rat	Wood	(+)
1925	25 January 1925 – 12 February 1926	Ox	Wood	(−)
1926	13 February 1926 – 1 February 1927	Tiger	Fire	(+)
1927	2 February 1927 – 22 January 1928	Rabbit	Fire	(−)
1928	23 January 1928 – 9 February 1929	Dragon	Earth	(+)
1929	10 February 1929 – 29 January 1930	Snake	Earth	(−)
1930	30 January 1930 – 16 February 1931	Horse	Metal	(+)
1931	17 February 1931 – 5 February 1932	Sheep	Metal	(−)
1932	6 February 1932 – 25 January 1933	Monkey	Water	(+)
1933	26 January 1933 – 13 February 1934	Rooster	Water	(−)
1934	14 February 1934 – 3 February 1935	Dog	Wood	(+)
1935	4 February 1935 – 23 January 1936	Pig	Wood	(−)
1936	24 January 1936 – 10 February 1937	Rat	Fire	(+)
1937	11 February 1937 – 30 January 1938	Ox	Fire	(−)
1938	31 January 1938 – 18 February 1939	Tiger	Earth	(+)
1939	19 February 1939 – 7 February 1940	Rabbit	Earth	(−)
1940	8 February 1940 – 26 January 1941	Dragon	Metal	(+)
1941	27 January 1941 – 14 February 1942	Snake	Metal	(−)
1942	15 February 1942 – 4 February 1943	Horse	Water	(+)
1943	5 February 1943 – 24 January 1944	Sheep	Water	(−)
1944	25 January 1944 – 12 February 1945	Monkey	Wood	(+)
1945	13 February 1945 – 1 February 1946	Rooster	Wood	(−)
1946	2 February 1946 – 21 January 1947	Dog	Fire	(+)
1947	22 January 1947 – 9 February 1948	Pig	Fire	(−)

YEAR	FROM – TO	ANIMAL SYMBOL	ELEMENT	ASPECT
1948	10 February 1948 – 28 January 1949	Rat	Earth	(+)
1949	29 January 1949 – 16 February 1950	Ox	Earth	(−)
1950	17 February 1950 – 5 February 1951	Tiger	Metal	(+)
1951	6 February 1951 – 26 January 1952	Rabbit	Metal	(−)
1952	27 January 1952 – 13 February 1953	Dragon	Water	(+)
1953	14 February 1953 – 2 February 1954	Snake	Water	(−)
1954	3 February 1954 – 16 February 1955	Horse	Wood	(+)
1955	24 January 1955 – 11 February 1956	Sheep	Wood	(−)
1956	12 February 1956 – 30 January 1957	Monkey	Fire	(+)
1957	31 January 1957 – 17 February 1958	Rooster	Fire	(−)
1958	18 February 1958 – 7 February 1959	Dog	Earth	(+)
1959	8 February 1959 – 27 January 1960	Pig	Earth	(−)
1960	28 January 1960 – 14 February 1961	Rat	Metal	(+)
1961	15 February 1961 – 4 February 1962	Ox	Metal	(−)
1962	5 February 1962 – 24 January 1963	Tiger	Water	(+)
1963	25 January 1963 – 12 February 1964	Rabbit	Water	(−)
1964	13 February 1964 – 1 February 1965	Dragon	Wood	(+)
1965	2 February 1965 – 20 January 1966	Snake	Wood	(−)
1966	21 January 1966 – 8 February 1967	Horse	Fire	(+)
1967	9 February 1967 – 29 January 1968	Sheep	Fire	(−)
1968	30 January 1968 – 16 February 1969	Monkey	Earth	(+)
1969	17 February 1969 – 5 February 1970	Rooster	Earth	(−)
1970	6 February 1970 – 26 January 1971	Dog	Metal	(+)
1971	27 January 1971 – 15 January 1972	Pig	Metal	(−)
1972	16 January 1972 – 2 February 1973	Rat	Water	(+)
1973	3 February 1973 – 22 January 1974	Ox	Water	(−)
1974	23 January 1974 – 10 February 1975	Tiger	Wood	(+)
1975	11 February 1975 – 30 January 1976	Rabbit	Wood	(−)
1976	31 January 1976 – 17 February 1977	Dragon	Fire	(+)
1977	18 February 1977 – 6 February 1978	Snake	Fire	(−)
1978	7 February 1978 – 27 January 1979	Horse	Earth	(+)
1979	28 January 1979 – 15 February 1980	Sheep	Earth	(−)

YEAR	FROM – TO	ANIMAL SYMBOL	ELEMENT	ASPECT
1980	16 February 1980 – 4 February 1981	Monkey	Metal	(+)
1981	5 February 1981 – 24 January 1982	Rooster	Metal	(−)
1982	25 January 1982 – 12 February 1983	Dog	Water	(+)
1983	13 February 1983 – 1 February 1984	Pig	Water	(−)
1984	2 February 1984 – 19 February 1985	Rat	Wood	(+)
1985	20 February 1985 – 8 February 1986	Ox	Wood	(−)
1986	9 February 1986 – 28 January 1987	Tiger	Fire	(+)
1987	29 January 1987 – 16 February 1988	Rabbit	Fire	(−)
1988	17 February 1988 – 5 February 1989	Dragon	Earth	(+)
1989	6 February 1989 – 26 January 1990	Snake	Earth	(−)
1990	27 January 1990 – 14 February 1991	Horse	Metal	(+)
1991	15 February 1991 – 3 February 1992	Sheep	Metal	(−)
1992	4 February 1992 – 22 January 1993	Monkey	Water	(+)
1993	23 January 1993 – 9 February 1994	Rooster	Water	(−)
1994	10 February 1994 – 30 January 1995	Dog	Wood	(+)
1995	31 January 1995 – 18 February 1996	Pig	Wood	(−)
1996	19 February 1996 – 7 February 1997	Rat	Fire	(+)
1997	8 February 1997 – 27 January 1998	Ox	Fire	(−)
1998	28 January 1998 – 5 February 1999	Tiger	Earth	(+)
1999	6 February 1999 – 27 January 2000	Rabbit	Earth	(−)
2000	5 February 2000 – 23 January 2001	Dragon	Metal	(+)
2001	24 January 2001 – 11 February 2002	Snake	Metal	(−)
2002	12 February 2002 – 31 January 2003	Horse	Water	(+)
2003	1 February 2003 – 21 January 2004	Sheep	Water	(−)
2004	22 January 2004 – 8 February 2005	Monkey	Wood	(+)
2005	8 February 2005 – 28 January 2006	Rooster	Wood	(−)
2006	29 January 2006 – 17 February 2007	Dog	Fire	(+)
2007	18 February 2007 – 6 February 2008	Pig	Fire	(−)

Chapter 2

ANIMAL INSTINCTS

The characteristics of each year sign

This chapter describes the twelve signs in turn together with their character keynotes, main personality traits, characteristics of the parent and child, relationships, emotional make-up, patterns of health and careers, hobbies and pastimes likely to suit.

Of course it must be constantly borne in mind that each person, whilst belonging to a particular sign, is nevertheless uniquely individual – a factor which is reflected in the complex levels of this fascinating system. The personality profiles that outline each lunar sign necessarily describe a pure type, whilst in reality it would be extremely rare to encounter an individual who fits the bill exactly. Having said that, though, it is uncanny how members of the same sign do seem to share similar characteristics, similar tastes and temperaments, similar likes, dislikes, hopes and aspirations, that distinguish them from members of the other eleven categories.

No Chinese astrologer would dream of making character assessments or, come to that, predictions, on the compatibility of two people simply by looking at the sign influencing the year in which they were born. Indeed, for every rule that may be laid down in this simplistic form of comparison there will be at the very least half a dozen couples ready to disprove it.

When it comes to the question of working out the likelihood of the compatibility of two people, therefore, an astrologer would have to take a good deal more than merely the animal sign into consideration. For example, the element which governs the year, the season, and the very hour of birth all contribute to the final equation. So, though Chinese astrology is adamant that, for example, a Tiger and an Ox would conflict, this rule would apply only to a Tiger and an Ox conforming to the pure types. Modified respectively by, say, the Pig and the Dog hour of birth and both belonging to, perhaps, the Water element, not only fundamentally changes the character of each individual but also changes the odds on the likely success rate of a relationship together.

So, by taking all the different levels into consideration, it is possible to make more accurate character analyses, predictions for the future and assessments of compatibility. When it comes to matching couples, then, if there are enough points of agreement, enough love, understanding and tolerance between the two, their relationship is likely to be a success, whether their lunar signs are overtly compatible or not.

To erect a full horoscope for an individual necessarily takes time and a good deal of experience. However, the beauty of the Chinese system is that even without having to delve too deeply, the animal sign governing an individual's year of birth will still yield an immense amount of information on every aspect of that person's make-up. Moreover, it will also reveal pathways and directions as a guide in which the individual may steer his or her life in the future.

THE RAT

Keynotes to Character: Sociable, pleasant, agreeable, amusing, charming, quick learner, sharp-witted.

The Sign: The Rat is the sign of charm.

Personality:
The Chinese Astrological cycle begins with the year of the Rat consequently those born within this category like to be first, pioneers, leaders of men, at the forefront of the action. Because of this, they tend to see themselves as a cut above the others. The top five percent, the crème de la crème, is the way in which these people have been known to refer to themselves. And, as leaders, they carry about them a somewhat majestic air for they are rather regal creatures who do well in any situation where they can be respected and looked up to.

Restless and inquisitive, those born under the influence of the Rat are active, both physically and mentally, and tend to lead busy lives. Challenge is essential to them for they love the thrill of living dangerously, of walking on a knife's edge. Travelling is one of their favourite pastimes for here they have the opportunity to explore distant horizons, to experiment with new sensations, to hone their senses with new experiences.

Back home, because Rats hate above all else the dull tedium of routine in life, they amass around themselves a variety of interests to keep their minds stimulated. Thus, people from this group will characteristically be found to have a stack of projects constantly on the boil so that when they become bored with one, they can leave that simmering whilst they go off and stir one or two of their other pots.

Rats are best known for their charm. Blessed with a sharp wit, they possess a marvellous sense of humour, which makes them stimulating and amusing company to have around. Generally extroverted, they may well be described as opportunists for they tend to prefer to live off their wits rather than labour long and hard to earn their daily bread.

It is to their advantage that these people are not only imaginative but also perceptive, able to see things objectively and to size up people and situations in the twinkling of an eye. Their sharp intuition guides them through for they possess far-reaching minds that see goals and ambitions in distant horizons and, typically single-minded, they go straight for the target.

Indeed, Rats are highly ambitious and although they do seem to have an eye to the main chance they are, nevertheless, prepared to put in a greal deal of practical hard work in order to reach their objective. And reach it they will, there is no doubt of that because, just as they like being first, they equally like being top.

In their dealings with others it is their extrovert natures that come to the fore for Rats love to make an impact, to leave a favourable impression of themselves indelibly imprinted in people's minds. But in truth there's little chance of forgetting these warm-hearted, affable folk whose very presence is the embodiment of charm.

On the domestic front, they are home-loving, sensuous creatures for whom comfort is of the essence. Sometimes generous to a fault and at other times frugal with their money they are, nevertheless, tenacious not only in spirit but also about their possessions. But their whole attitude to money does pose a certain ambiguity in their natures because although they may be careful and prudent about some things, when it comes to the purchase of paintings, books and objets d'art they will spend money as if there were no tomorrow. Equally, they are prepared to buy expensive gifts and simply lavish money on those they love. Funny thing is, when it comes to the basic needs of living or, for that matter, when it concerns people the Rats do not like, they can be quite parsimonious but, when it comes to the enjoyment of the senses and people they do like, spending is quite a different matter!

And talking about the people they love, loyalty is a particular characteristic of this sign and Rats are especially renowned for standing by their loved ones and for sticking up for their friends.

But when unhappy or when confronted with difficulties in life, Rats are not able to accept the situation gracefully nor indeed philosophically and at those times they will become fretful and obsessive, irritatingly fussing and niggling over trifling details. And, though tolerant and fairly easy-going in general, there is always a feeling of an implicit sense of aggression lurking just under the surface, and the hint that if seriously rubbed up the wrong way, that anger might break through their wonderful charm and ease of manner.

In essence, though, Rats may be considered as lucky

types and, with their quick wits and broad-minded approach, they generally enjoy life's broad canvas, delight in experiencing all sorts of new sensations and get as much out of life as they possibly can.

The Rat lover: Rats are able to control their feelings and will generally present a cool facade to the outside world, regardless of whatever volcanic emotions they may be feeling inside. But these are passionate creatures whose feelings can be deeply stirred and though able to control them as a rule, when the volcano does erupt, watch out! Perhaps one of their faults is their inability to actually talk about their feelings to those they love, and consequently they tend to repress them – thus adding to the volcanic pressure. As well as being deeply passionate these are sensual creatures who simply exude sexuality and who greatly enjoy all forms of physical stimulation.

The Rat parent: Rats make good, warm-hearted, spontaneous parents. They have plenty of wit and good humour which they readily use to diffuse any potentially explosive problem. Because Rats are so broad-minded, they tend to favour as wide and as liberal an education for their children as possible. Adventurous themselves, they enjoy joining in their offsprings' imaginative games, encouraging both mental and physical exploration. But there are times when the Rat's keen mental powers will lose patience if their children display a lazy mind or are uninterested academically; then the Rat's short-temper will explode.

The Rat child: Childhood for the young Rat is perhaps the happiest time of their life. From a very early age they will show an aptitude for sports and games and a love for the outdoor life. As children they are inquisitive and consequently eager to learn, to explore their environment, and expand their awareness. At school, Rat children may excel in languages and if they are academic and choose to go on to higher education, chances are they will choose humanities or literature studies. Generally speaking, this group make keen students who are always ready to pick up new skills.

Health: Rats are wiry and tenacious and never give in to ill-health. If they are ever ill, they will simply fight their way back to health again. People born under this influence need to watch their sweet tooth or they may put on weight. Old age seems to be a time of peace and contentment for this group but, ominously, according to legend Rats tend to die a sudden death.

Careers, hobbies and pastimes: Writing, acting, music, arts and handicrafts, anything to do with the theatre, sports and travel.

THE OX

Keynotes to Character: Trustworthy, reliable, strong-willed, plodding, orderly, organised.

The Sign: The Ox is the sign of industry.

Personality:
When it comes to constancy, to perseverance and to endurance, there are no other members of the Chinese Zodiac who can match those born in the year of the Ox. These strong personalities are solid, stolid characters who might be described as possessing true grit. Thoroughly trustworthy and dependable, they are blessed with cast-iron integrity and never shrink from donning the mantle of responsibility.

People born under the influence of the Ox are kind, caring souls, logical, positive, filled with common-sense and with their feet firmly planted on the ground. Security is their main preoccupation in life and they are prepared to beaver away, to toil long and hard in order to provide a warm, comfortable and stable nest for themselves and their families.

Indeed, once these people have secured around themselves a home, a supportive partner and a loving family, they will contentedly plough their furrow, slowly and carefully building up their skills, reputation and expertise in their chosen field in life.

They are not, however, quite as bovine as their initial description might suggest. Strong-minded, stubborn, individualistic, the majority, in fact, are highly intelligent individuals who don't take kindly to being told what to do.

And at home Oxen are especially dominant types with extremely high standards of excellence which can make them rather difficult to live with. They like to make the rules and woe betide those who step out of line! As they grow older they have a tendency to become more conservative with age, more unyielding, inflexible and rigid in their outlook, so they are the ones, according to Chinese legend, who are most in danger of ending up alone in later life unless they learn to be more tolerant of those around them.

In the work-place Oxen carry out their duties quietly, steadily and methodically with no great dramatic gestures. Not the sort to put themselves forward, they don't particularly go for centre stage, but prefer to quietly work away in the wings. Yet, when necessary, they can bring forth qualities of leadership for beneath their quiet exterior they possess a commanding presence, an ability to take charge and a voice to be reckoned with. And, because they tend to brook no nonsense, they find they are able not only to get others to toe the line, but also to inspire loyalty and respect for their even-handed and fair-minded way of dealing with things.

Indeed, it would be fair to say that, although Ox people don't ask to be put in the limelight, they do nevertheless, like to be boss for these quietly dominant types enjoy being in positions of power. And, even though they may not broadcast their virtues to the world, nevertheless it is that steady, conscientious attitude that will, sooner or later, deservedly see them to the top.

Though ostensibly practical, conservative and traditional, Ox people, and particularly the ladies, know how to present themselves when it comes to grand occasions and will always turn out 'comme il faut' with sophistication and aplomb. Classical outfits, beautifully and elegantly tailored, especially suit this group rather than the ephemeral fashions. Besides, Ox folk have a knack of personalising anything they wear, so whether modern or classical they will always turn out stylishly and completely individualistic.

The Ox lover: Oxen make solid, steady, reliable partners. Very affectionate to those close to their hearts, they are, nevertheless, cool and distant to anyone outside their emotional circle. In fact, getting close to an Ox is a very difficult thing to do for they hold all but their chosen few at arms length. But, once they have committed themselves, they make loyal, steadfast lovers and the least likely, of all the animal signs, to possess a roving eye. Indeed, casual love affairs are definitely not in the Oxen style of things. As lovers, they have been accused of lacking romance but make no mistake, though they may not show it, their emotions are deep and passionate. And if their love is spurned, or if they should suffer a broken heart, they will retreat inside themselves and channel all their emotions into their work. An Ox, happily settled in a contented relation ship, will make a supportive and faithful partner, someone whose love grows stronger by the year and whose sterling qualities are worth his/her weight in gold.

The Ox parent: Ox parents are committed and devoted to their offspring and thus make very good mothers and fathers. Females of this group especially feel the mothering instinct from a very early age. But before they even start their families they like to build solid and secure foundations into which to bring up their children. As parents they are considered disciplinarians and noted for their firm guidance but they are also fair-minded. However, their children must toe the line and learn not to overstep the mark otherwise all hell will be let loose. Ox parents are conservative in their beliefs about education just as they are conservative in all other areas of life, consequently they will want their children to follow a solid and traditional type of education.

The Ox child: Childhood for Ox individuals is not usually an easy time. Many are shy youngsters, reserved and often lonely, whether because they are only children or because there is a wide discrepancy in the ages of their brothers and sisters. Thrown to themselves they learn to become independent, self-resourceful and responsible from a very young age. At school, Ox children are prepared to work hard and often show an aptitude for practical as well as for creative subjects. Their quiet respectful attitudes and qualities of leadership will often shine through and they will find themselves rewarded by being placed into positions of responsibility even when still quite young.

Health: People who are born under the influence of the Ox are generally robust individuals who don't, as a rule, suffer with ill-health. They must ensure, however, that they get plenty of exercise and fresh air throughout their lives for this group can become quite complacent, especially as they get older, and they will consequently find that their health could seriously suffer as a result of weight problems and loss of fitness. Despite this, however, Oxen are considered to enjoy long life.

Careers, hobbies and pastimes: At work, Oxen like to feel part of a large organisation. Many will be found working in institutions, corporations, hospitals, colleges and universities. Team sports attract young Oxen whilst older ones get a kick out of gardening. Creative and artistic projects of all sorts, handicrafts and D.I.Y. are all typical Oxen activities.

THE TIGER

Keynotes to Character: Dynamic, energetic, competitive, assertive, active, charismatic, spontaneous.

The Sign: The Tiger is the sign of bravery and daring.

Personality:
Tigers like to be in charge. They are born with an innate ability to take command of any situation, to take the running of the show into their own hands. Unlike the Oxen, born in the year preceding their own, these people don't quietly wait on the sidelines but have the sort of personalities that must always assert themselves, that must always take centre stage, whatever the circumstances.

For a start, they like to choose their own destiny regardless of what others tell them to do. Immensely individualistic, they have a compulsion to make their own rules in life because taking orders from others is complete anathema to them. Furthermore, they have what might be described as a cavalier attitude to life, vast sweeping gestures are more in their style, nit-picking red tape or dotting 'i's' and crossing 't's', certainly is NOT.

The most outstanding quality associated with this group is courage. Tigers are fearless creatures in as much as they blind themselves to dangers and impetuously rush in where more cautious individuals would think at least twice first. Outspoken in the face of injustice, their strong humanitarian instincts will not allow them to pass by if they see a wrong perpetrated upon another. In true Quixotic fashion, if they believe in a good cause they will champion it without thought of the consequences to themselves. When they have wind of the chase they will pursue their quarry with intensity and when they get their teeth in they simply won't let go, regardless of any danger that may befall them in the process.

A dynamic personality, the Tiger will always leave a vortex of activity and excitement in their train. These people have an abundance of energy which they will use in almost frantic bursts that sweep everyone and everything along in the enthusiasm of the moment. Indeed, there is rarely a dull moment when Tigers are around.

The snag is that such high-octane bursts of energy cannot be sustained for long periods of time and thus they may all too easily burn themselves out. Fortunately, there are plenty of resources in the seemingly bottom-less Tiger pit and after a short spell of rest and recuperation, these people will simply bounce straight back on the scene with renewed vigour and just as much explosive excitement and enthusiasm as before.

Tigers have an inborn magnetic personality that attracts people to them like bees to honey. Warm-hearted, sociable and friendly, they are characterised by their frank, honest and open approach. Not famed for beating about the bush, their friends will need to shore up their sensitivities because when these out-front individuals want something, they will simply ask for it directly. But their immense kindness and generosity will always shine through except, of course, when crossed or backed into a corner, for then they can become vehement and ferocious. And if they, or one of their loved ones, should be threatened, make no mistake about it, these people will go straight for the jugular.

Temperamentally, Tigers can be volatile and unpredictable, aspects of their personality which make them so exciting to have around. Hot-headed, they are renowned for possessing a very short fuse. Impatient, rebellious, impetuous and unrestrained, they go through life with unshakeable optimism, cocking a snook at convention whenever they can.

Yet, despite their non-conformity these, above all the other signs, possess a high degree of self-reflection together with a heightened sense of awareness, so they are ever ready to learn by their mistakes. Indeed, they are excellent at self-learning, for they can pick things up at a glance and teach themselves anything they put their minds to by reading it up in books or simply by observing others at a task.

Tigers are indeed likeable people and will always have a wide following because, despite all else, the quality that most comes across is a charming wide-eyed naïvety about life, a conviction that good will triumph against evil and a firm adherence to the old-fashioned code of honour, of chivalry, of consideration and good manners towards others. With such an outlook on life it is difficult not to turn a blind eye to their faults.

The Tiger lover: Tigers make ardent and virile lovers. Because of their sensuality, their impetuousness and love of adventure, there is a frisson of excitement that not only follows Tigers wherever they go, but also guarantees them a certain irresistible sexy allure. Needless to say, these creatures whose emotions are outfront, have strong libidos and are lusty in their passions. Generally flirtatious, they are especially prone to wild flings in their early years but do settle down as they get older. When committed to a happy and fulfilling relationship, these people make loving and caring partners, warm-hearted and generous. They don't, however, lose that romantic streak, nor that exciting ability to surprise.

The Tiger parent: Tigers make excellent parents. No mother or father could be courageous, more defensive and, if need be, more aggressive, in the caring and protection of their child. Exciting and stimulating, they are always prepared to try out new theories, new ideas and will sweep their children along in their enthusiasm. And if their offspring should take up a new hobby or bring home a project from school, the Tiger parent is likely to get quite carried away in the excitement of joining in. Open-minded and non-conformist themselves, they are able to understand any rebellious tendencies in their young, but they WILL NOT brook bad behaviour or discourtesy from them towards others. They believe in teaching their children by their own example, or by putting views and lessons on life across in story-form, especially if there's a moral or two tucked away somewhere in the tale.

The Tiger child: Little Tigers make bright, friendly and affectionate children, ever inventive and full of life and of bright ideas. They are boisterous, noisy and competitive with no less energy and enthusiasm for life than their adult counterparts. With their sunny and outgoing natures, they easily make friends and soon become popular amongst their peers. Quick to learn and to catch on, they have a Peter-Pan excitement about life that leads them to ask interminable questions and that gives them a driving desire to explore to the very limits of their environment and their experience. They can be stubborn and headstrong, prone to outbursts of temper and to sudden changes of mood – unless taught from a very early age the value of compromise. As they grow in understanding, many develop a tendency to kick out against authority, to rebel against conventions, against rules and regulations. Consequently, in carving out their own destiny for themselves, some could well go against the wishes of their parents, drop out or experiment for a time with a Bohemian way of life.

Health: Tigers generally enjoy good, vigorous health. They do, however, need to learn to pace themselves so that they use their energies more consistently rather than over-stretch their resources in great swoops of activity that then leaves them exhausted and in need of recuperation.

Careers, hobbies and pastimes: People born in the year of the Tiger make first rate actors but, if this is out of the question as a main career, then amateur dramatics in their spare time would suit them admirably. Fast-action sports will always attract this group, the excitement of the race-course and the lure of the motor-racing track will be irrestible to them.

THE RABBIT

Keynotes to Character: Creative, garrulous, sociable, generous, conciliatory, peace-loving, sometimes remote.

The Sign: The Rabbit is the sign of peace, of grace and of family life.

Personality:
People born in the year of the Rabbit are characterised by their peace-loving nature. These people are great pacifists, loathing anything to do with violence and brutality and war. They will avoid physical conflict for as long as possible, subscribing wholeheartedly to the Churchillian view that 'jaw not war' should be the way of resolving one's differences. And it is because of this very philosophy that Rabbit folk make such good negotiators and diplomats, every ready to pour oil over troubled waters, to find a compromise that will satisfy all concerned.

But, although pacifists at heart, Rabbits do not lack

courage and if, when all peaceable solutions have been tried and failed, the situation still requires physical confrontation then Rabbits will fight as bravely as the next man in order to uphold their principles and protect all that they feel is dear to them.

Even greater than their love of peace, however, or their courage come to that, is their wisdom. For Rabbits seem to be born with an innate sagacity, a natural shrewdness which makes them street-wise when it comes to the affairs of the world. Intuitive and with a canny understanding, they seem to possess an ability to see things before they happen, a talent which secures them the best deals both in business and in life, whilst also ensuring them financial stability and security.

With their natural instinct for mothering, it is domesticity, love of the family, nurturing life, that are the type of activities most suited to the Rabbit. For them, home may be described as the centre of the universe, for everything revolves around family life. And because their places of abode are so very important they take a great deal of pleasure in making their houses warm, comfortable and stylish.

Indeed style, as well as an eye for beauty, are especially associated with this group whose members in general possess refined tastes together with artistic skills. Highly creative people, art is of particular interest to them. Whether it is that they can paint or sketch in their own right or that they have a strong appreciation for works of art many, because of the Rabbit's built-in acquisitive nature, become great collectors, filling their houses with beautiful paintings and objets d'art.

Their creativity, together with their sensitivity, another attribute of the Rabbit, means that they also appreciate music, some even becoming accomplished musicians.

Rabbits are described as cold individuals, rather stand-offish types who dislike physical contact with others. But try not to be put off by the Rabbit's aloofness because, as those who have been closely associated with these individuals will have long understood, this coolness is simply a means of masking their deeply sensitive nature.

But that sensitivity may also account, and be responsible, for the Rabbit's notorious moodiness, a tendency to swing from elation to depression at the drop of a hat.

Like Oxen, method, order and routine are essential to the well-being of Rabbit folk. They need a carefully planned existence because once their routine is upset, these creatures will be all at sixes and sevens – a state of affairs that will completely unnerve and unsettle people belonging to this group.

Sociability is important to the Rabbit not only in terms of being friendly and chatty – make no mistake about it, these can be very garrulous people! – but also in the cultivation of manners and the social graces. In whatever walk of life members of this group find themselves, they will always be distinguished by their sense of refinement and their cultured views. Elegant both physically and intellectually, Rabbits will always stand out from the crowd either as extremly stylish dressers or because they create an individualistic fashion statement of their own.

The Rabbit lover: Though Rabbits are sensitive, sentimental creatures, emotional and easily moved to tears, when it comes to committing themselves to a long-term relationship, they can be quite mercenary. Their driving passion is a desire for an easy life, filled with as much comfort and luxury as they can get. Thus they are more likely to show their allegiance to someone who will not only provide security and stability but who will also guarantee as much of la dolce vita as they can. But to give them their due, once they have found the right partner, they make faithful husbands or wives, dedicated home-makers, devoting themselves to their families and to their homes. And, by the way, their sensuality usually ensures that the Rabbit family will be a large one.

The Rabbit parent: Rabbits often have large families, which is just as well because they do have a deeply sensual nature and are known to be rather libidinous types. Indeed, the procreative habits of this furry little creature are quite legendary! But to give them their due, though they may be sensual, they are in general very faithful to their partners. As parents, they make excellent teachers to their young, strongly protective but also fairly possessive too. Yet they can come across as possibly a little remote to their children, a little too emotionally cool and distant.

The Rabbit child: Rabbit children are in general well-behaved and easy to bring up but noticeably tender and sensitive. As a sign, these are very emotional people, easily moved and even when young they stand out as rather prone to crying. Both boys and girls have a strong attachment to their mothers to the point where boys may be unkindly labelled as 'mummy's boys', or considered to be 'tied to their mother's apron-strings'. And because of that soft inner core they learn very early on to mask their sensitivities and to build a protective barrier that will shield their feelings from the outside world.

Health: Rabbits are said to enjoy longevity. However, the biggest problem for Rabbits is that they are not able to deal with stress very well. Members of other signs may actively enjoy the sudden surge of adrenalin that comes from confrontational situations, and even get a positive charge out of it. But not so those born during the year of the Rabbit because for these, living or working under too much stress or pressure, is the quickest way of endangering their health. For the Rabbit, then, tranquility is the essence of good health and well-being.

Careers, hobbies and professions: Any domestic activity will suit those born in the year of the Rabbit: cookery, handicrafts, sewing, knitting, embroidery, D.I.Y., sketching, painting, playing musical instruments are all Rabbit-oriented subjects. Building up a family business or working in an already established family concern suits this group right down to the ground. Otherwise, vocational or community work attract many members of this sign. Politics, and in particular the Diplomatic Corps, are ideal Rabbit occupations.

THE DRAGON

Keynotes to Character: Refined, self-assured, full of vitality, superficial, unusual.

The Sign: The Dragon is the sign of luck and good fortune.

Personality:
There is a decidedly exotic air about Dragon people, especially amongst the women, who fairly exude sexuality. Indeed, whether male or female, Dragons are libidinous and score quite a hit with the opposite sex.

Flexible and accommodating, they fit in with whatever is going on around them – but for only as long as it suits them. This is because they are pretty self-determined types and don't take kindly to being dominated by others. In fact, though seemingly affable and agreeable, they can be as ferocious and dangerous as the mythical beast on whom the sign is based. Powerful creatures these, when they sense treachery they will belch enough fire to burn up any opposition or enmity that might be levelled at their heads.

In general, though, they are kind and generous friends as long as, that is, they are allowed to take the lead. In fact, Dragons are often found in positions of authority and power because they like to be in charge. Taking orders and having to toe the line is anathema to these people who are much happier and healthier when running the show themselves than when relegated to the supporting cast. Indeed, historically in China the Dragon represented power, and in particular, it stood for the power and magnificence of the Emperor. And it is this very splendour that is associated with people born under its influence.

Intellectually, they are clever, bright, sharp people, yet it is found that on occasion they will throw all logic to the wind and follow their hunches. Fortunately for them, they are strong on intuition and invariably all works out well. Interestingly, no matter what surprises fate may have in store, whatever difficulties or hardships these people may encounter along the road, Dragons will always land on their feet.

This is undoubtedly due to the fact that of the Chinese signs, those born under the influence of the Dragon are the luckiest of all and good fortune simply follows them wherever they go. Not only that, they also have the Midas touch. The Year of the Dragon, it is said, is good for business and all money-making schemes. Consequently, those born in this year have an inherent knack for attracting money and they generally enjoy financial prosperity.

And because of their easy-come attitude to money, Dragons make very generous people to have around. Indeed, it is most unusual to come across a Dragon who is a skinflint. These people, then, tend to spend money freely – though sometimes there is a tendency for it to go out just as quickly as it comes in!

Open, honest and forthright, one of their short-comings is that they expect others to be as out-front as themselves. They lack guile and deviousness and as such are in danger of falling into traps that other, more Machiavellian, individuals set for them and, caught off their guard, they can find that before too long they are being stabbed in the back.

These, however, are multi-talented creatures who possess an especially original turn of mind. They can be ingenious and resourceful and so have the capacity to make remarkable come-backs. No-one can but marvel at the indomitable spirit which enables them to pick themselves up when they are down, whether physically, psychologically or materially, and power their way meteorically from rags to riches, right back up to the top of the ladder. Remember, Dragons never say die and never accept defeat, and their positive, thrusting nature makes sure they will be there to fight another day.

Temperamentally, Dragons are somewhat hot-headed and quick-tempered; when angered they will give as good as they get. In fact, it is not really advisable to cross swords with a Dragon unless the opponent is another Dragon. And another drawback of this sign is a lack of sensitivity, for Dragons can be hyper-critical if things aren't quite right or not up to their expectations. They don't choose their words too carefully either when they make their anger or disappointment known!

In their younger days Dragons may lack a certain confidence in themselves but, once they have found their feet, they can all too often swing the other way and become quite conceited with a blown-up sense of self-importance. And it is this negative trait in their character which can all too easily attract enemies.

In general, though, people born in a Dragon year are popular, and they don't have to work hard at being liked – they just are – which is a jolly good thing for them because these, more than any other category, have a huge need to be loved. Strong, powerful, extrovert, self-reliant, these are charismatic individuals who make their presence felt and who bring with them wherever they go a little bit of magic, a little bit of glamour and quite a few fireworks to lighten the gloom and liven up the proceedings. Indeed, the resplendent Dragon is able to fill the world with colour from what appears to be a magic paintbox which never seems to run dry.

The Dragon lover: There are two types of Dragon lovers; those who fall in love and commit themselves to a serious relationship when they are fairly young, and those who tend to be loners and perhaps never marry at all. In general, the former enjoy a stable and satisfactory married life whilst the latter flit from one love affair to another, never really giving any of them a chance to develop. Indeed, many committed bachelors and spinsters are born under the influence of this sign. In any partnership Dragon folk will first and foremost be seeking an intellectual rapport for these people get as much charge from the mental stimulation as they do from having sex. And, of course, they bring to any relationship their own inimitable touch of magic and that Dragon element of good fortune. But the male Dragon is perhaps happier in love than his female counterpart, for this, being a strongly masculine sign, often produces dominant women who tend to take over the relationship and rather blindly tread all over the sensitivities of their partners.

The Dragon parent: Parenting does not come naturally to this group. Work seems to take up such a lot of the Dragon's time and energy that many don't marry at all and don't find the time to start a family. Those who do have children, however, have a strong sense of duty and responsibility towards them and, true to their nature, make generous mothers and fathers. Perhaps, though, that generosity is given more in material terms rather than giving of themselves or of their time to their youngsters.

The Dragon child: Dragon children are often lonely youngsters, withdrawn and as a result may be misunderstood. Many take time to find their feet and simply lack self-confidence during their early years. But they possess wonderful imaginations and should be gently encouraged to believe in themselves and in their many gifts and talents. On the other hand, with the right backing, with praise and with positive guidance little Dragons can shine. Indeed, if one were to take a count, it would be astonishing to find how many child stars come from this category – Shirley Temple, the young Yehudi Menuhin and our own Bonnie Langford, to name but three. The more independent Dragons seem to be born with an old head on their young shoulders and will appreciate being given responsibilities and treated like an adult even from a very early age.

Health: In general, it is said that Dragon-born individuals enjoy a long life.

Careers, hobbies and pastimes: Work-wise, Dragons are famed for their charm; in fact these people could charm the birds from the trees. As such they make first rate salesmen and women, are brilliant in PR and in advertising. Interestingly, Dragons are also drawn to New Age subjects, to alternative or complementary studies and interests which might be described as occult in nature.

Music appeals to Dragons of all ages and so do sports – as long as the Dragon can be team leader. Perhaps, then, sporting activities where the person can shine as an individual would be preferred. Tennis, running, horse-riding, single canoeing would all suit. If they can, these people travel extensively and get a great charge from visiting different countries and enjoy new environments and new atmospheres immensely.

THE SNAKE

Keynotes to Character: Cautious, prudish, mysterious, sometimes sagacious and sometimes ingenious.

The Sign: The Snake is the sign of wisdom.

Personality:
Personality-wise, Snakes are not people who can be easily ignored. They possess a strong, charismatic presence and a charm which has been described by some astrologers as 'bewitching' or 'beguiling'.

People born during the year of the Snake are said to be endowed with wisdom and with deep philosophical understanding. In matters of business they can be shrewd, biding their time in making a deal only to strike like lightning and make a killing when they judge the moment is right. Thus in life, the majority of Snakes are financially successful and generally lucky with money. However, if they rush at their decisions, gamble rashly or if they don't follow their instincts, they can be spectacularly unlucky for their fortunes very much depend on their careful and considered judgement in financial affairs and on their intuitive feelings in business negotiations.

In general, these are serious types, deep thinkers who could never be considered shallow or frivolous. In fact, there is an almost inexplicable ponderousness to their characters, the weight of centuries on their shoulders which some have been led to believe is their karmic lot. Indeed, many Snakes are driven by a sense of inner purpose, a mission in life, a strong sense of destiny, history in the making through their very actions in the world.

These are clever, intelligent people who take time to formulate their ideas and opinions. When they give their advice which, on the whole, they have probably deliberated on long and hard, it is always worth listening to, if not even following wholesale. And even when they are at their laziest, for subjects of this sign do have a reputation for sluggishness, their minds are working ten to the dozen, laying their schemes and hatching their plots for the future.

They command respect yet, perhaps because of their fundamentally unpredictable natures, one can't help being rather circumspect when around them. And it would indeed be wise to be cautious in any undertaking where Snakes are involved because there are times when they can be treacherous creatures who delight in intrigue and who wouldn't think twice about double-crossing someone in order to save their own skins. And their quietly calculating natures will never forgive nor forget a slight and though it may seem that they have forgotten, they will wait patiently until they are good and ready and then, when their adversary is least expecting it, they will sink in their venomous fangs in one lethal blow.

Indeed, there is a certain duality about Snake

individuals which makes them somewhat untenable. Sometimes they will appear strong and ready for action and then at another time they will be cautious and calculating. Sometimes they come across as full of wisdom and then again there is more than a hint of naïvety about them. Just like the symbol of their sign, natives of the Snake year make slippery customers!

Subtle, secretive, elusive and enigmatic, there is an element of the mysterious that surrounds the Snake personality. Perhaps this is due to their strong intuitive faculties which enable them very often to put their fingers right on the button – for many of them are psychic. Or perhaps it is a consequence of their strong inner spirituality which can manifest itself in an interest in religion, mysticism or even in the occult. In fact, Snakes themselves possess all the ingredients that make a mystic.

And it is this inner sensitivity, too, that accounts for the Snake's appreciation of the Arts and especially music. Many show an extraordinary talent for playing a musical instrument and even if not accomplished musicians themselves, they will greatly enjoy and appreciate music throughout their lives. Art, too, is a passion. If they don't actually paint, they may well involve themselves in the world of art or at the very least collect and adorn their homes with the finest paintings and sculptures they can afford. Antiquaries and all manner of rare books, too, have a place in the Snake's household. Whenever possible Snakes will patronise artistic endeavours, enjoy going to concerts, to the theatre or to the opera. And wherever there may be an art exhibition, there will be a throng of Snakes to appreciate and, if possible, invest in the works.

In other respects, they are not generally considered extravagant. Indeed, though on the whole financially secure, they may have a tendency to penny-pinch except when it comes to adornments and embellishments for which the ladies of the sign have a great love. For example, Snake ladies will have quite a collection of good costume jewellery and accessories with which to ring the changes of their stylish clothes. Their jewellery, none the less, will be classy and expensive – there's no room for cheap and tawdry stuff on the Snake's dressing table.

And why not indeed, for Snakes are notoriously good looking and like to project the best image of themselves that they can. Both men and women of the sign have elegant and stylish tastes in clothes, the men are sexy and the ladies seductive. Hardly surprising, then, that these have been labelled self-centred and vain. To give them their due, however, whether in looks or in circumstances, Snakes simply have a magical knack of making the very best out of the most mediocre.

The Snake lover: The Snake personality is described as careful and, true to type, when it comes to the choice of a partner, these people are infinitely selective. For them, only the very best will do. Elegance will be one of the first attractions, but so too is good breeding and delicate manners. And, again true to type, when they find the partner of their dreams they will brook no opposition, allow nothing to stand in their way, until they win the heart of the object of their desire. Then, having won their prize, they become possessive and jealous, fearful that it should slip out of their hands. Deeply passionate, these are demanding lovers, highly sensual creatures, sexy in the extreme. Yet, neither male nor female Snake could possibly be described as butch or aggressive. The males of the sign are perhaps more inclined to be part of the New Man philosophy. And lady Snakes are ultra-feminine – sultry, exotic creatures, femmes fatales, in every sense of the word. Success and power will turn her on and she will probably make a bee-line for the richest and most influential person she can find.

The Snake parent: Because Snakes are such notoriously sensual people, they are likely to become deeply involved with several sexual partners throughout their lives. It is highly probable, then, that Snakes will find themselves parenting a host of step-children from their previous marriages. Lack of communication is perhaps the major pitfall of the Snake mother or father but their marvellous sense of humour, that ability to pick out the drole, the funny or sardonic side of any situation, no matter how difficult, will bring them through these most trying of moments that all parents have to face, whatever sign their offspring may be born under.

The Snake child: Snake children are, on the whole, late developers. Consequently they need lots of encouragement to get started, to find their talents and make them flourish. In a sense they can be their own worst enemies because they are secretive, prone to sulking when they don't get their own way and seemingly unable to talk about their feelings or explain their reasons and motivation to their family and teachers. Because of this difficulty with communication they are frequently loners and as such even more misunderstood. But they make good students, quick and intelligent learners and very soon pick up on the fact that turning on their charm makes it easier for them to get what they want in life.

Health: Snakes suffer with inner turmoil. When under stress they have a tendency to turn their tension inwards. When angered, they allow their passions to seethe inside and invariably it is their digestive systems which take the strain. So physiologically, the most vulnerable areas of the Snake are the stomach and intestines and those born under this influence are especially prone to duodenal ulcers. Psychologically, though generally emotionally stable, that inner turmoil can take its toll on the nervous system, resulting in conditions such as nervous exhaustion or, more seriously, in a total nervous breakdown.

Careers, hobbies and pastimes: Music and the Arts are especially Snake-type interests, whether for professional purposes or leisure activities. Subjects that may be classified as occult, as mystical arts or as Oriental philosophy may also appeal, especially if they are concerned with the analysis of character and with the deeper levels of understanding the human condition. For the same reasons philosophy, psychology, psychiatry and psychotherapy are suitable fields for the more academically-minded Snakes.

THE HORSE

Keynotes to Character: Strong, active, self-resourceful, self-centred, gregarious, narrow-minded.

The Sign: The Horse is the sign of refinement and fervour.

Personality:

Active strength perhaps describes members of this group in a nut-shell. These people have masses of physical resources. Strong and energetic, they like to be kept busy, to be on the go the whole time. And they are especially at their best in situations where their stamina and physical resources are put to the test.

People born during the year of the Horse have a pleasant, amiable, easy-going disposition, which guarantees popularity and a goodly following of friends. Blessed with good humour, geniality and bonhomie, they are extremely comfortable to get along with for they have the knack of instantly putting people at their ease.

Indeed, these people have a happy outlook – although sometimes their prolonged heartiness may grate just a little! But they are in general able to scatter their rays of sunshine about and bring a good deal of cheer to those around them.

Freedom and independence are as essential to Horse-born people as the air they breathe. A low boredom threshold, both in terms of interests and friendships, is characteristic of those belonging to this sign and adds a whimsical quality to the otherwise level-headedness of these folk. Consequently, they tend to act on impulse and, being their own masters and mistresses, this means that there is an element of unpredictability about them. Perhaps they will be late for that special appointment they swore they would keep and then again, perhaps they won't show up at all. But they are so affable and agreeable about the whole thing that you can't be cross with them for long. Besides, they can be so casual in their attitude to life that they wouldn't dream of keeping *you* to your word and they certainly wouldn't bear any resentment if you were unable to fulfil a commitment *you* had undertaken.

Yet despite their carefree outlook on life, they can be staunchly loyal to family and friends and, in times of need, thoroughly responsible and dependable. More-over, if they choose to, they will allow themselves to be saddled with responsibility with quite cheerful acceptance.

Like the symbol by which they are represented, Horse-born people are high-spirited and lively. Some-times rash and wilful, they can be prone to rapid changes of mood and although seldom really explosive of temper, when they do see red, it is not a pretty sight. Resourceful and self-confident, they approach all things enthusiastically, putting one-hundred-and-twenty percent of effort and energy into whatever they are doing.

Quick-witted and mentally alert, they are quick to catch on and efficient in all their undertakings. They have to be really because, what with being skittish and boredom setting in so quickly, they have to fit in as much as they can in a short space of time so that they can then go galloping off to pastures new. But they are people who can juggle many things at the same time, keeping several projects in the air whilst concentrating on those immediately to hand. And because of this ability, this dexterous and incisive mind of theirs, they can make accurate judgements in the sheer twinkling of an eye and sound decisions at the flick of their fingers. They are particularly skilled at handling money, very often in business dealings following their hunches. And right they are too, for when it comes to intuition they have a sixth-sense that is quite uncanny.

But flights of fancy, chasing tenuous intellectual concepts and fantastical imaginings are not part of the Horse nature at all. These are not day-dreamers but thoroughly practical types, logical and down-to-earth. Indeed, people of this group are never very far from terra firma – with the exception, that is, of when they fall in love.

Then they are vulnerable. In love, no member of the other eleven signs tends to lose his or her head quite so easily or turn to putty quite so readily. It is here that Horse-born individuals will show just how headstrong and independent they can be. Despite all the warnings, they rush in where others would fear to tread only to find when they're knee-deep that all the advice had been right all along, that the ardour and impetuosity were misplaced, and that once the relationship loses its initial excitement the same old boredom, the same familiarity that breeds contempt, sets in yet again.

All people born under this sign are highly diplomatic in their dealings with others. They can be so suave that one might be forgiven for thinking that they had all graduated from charm school. Some astrologers have even gone so far as to label them the playboys or the jet-setters of the Chinese Zodiac. Refinement and elegance are often associated with this group and in general these folk share a strong sense of dress and of style. They have a particular penchant for elegant clothes and they like to make a 'fashion statement'.

Quite the reverse of their preceding sign, the Snake, those born in the year of the Horse cannot keep their own counsel. Chatty and gossipy, they have to be about the most garrulous of the twelve. Thoughts and feelings and emotions simply pour out of their mouths in a steady stream. They are just unable to keep a secret even if it were to save their own lives. So be warned, sharing a confidence with a Horse-born person is the quickest way of broadcasting your business to the whole world.

The Horse lover: When they fall in love, Horses seem to lose all logic, all sense of perspective. Unpredictable at the best of times, when they lose their hearts, there is simply no telling what the Horse-born will do next. And this is a pity because they do seem to fall in love easily – in fact probably more times than most other signs – each time repeating the same old familiar story, that THIS time it's for keeps, THIS time it really IS Mr or Ms Right, though patently obvious to everyone else that it's just another mistake. Two reasons stand out for this apparent flighty behaviour. The first is that these people possess an extremely low boredom threshold and soon get tired of the same people and the same situations. The second is that they love their independence and as soon as they feel a partner is making too many demands, or limiting their freedom, they will kick out and rebel and then gallop off in search of pastures new. Age eventually mellows the Horse and those born under its influence who have not found stability when younger are likely to settle down in later life.

The Horse parent: Though Horses love their children very much they can find it difficult to verbally communicate their feelings to them. Consequently, Horse parents can often appear distant and remote from a child's point of view. Not only that, but Horses tend to put their work first and their loved ones second so that these parents may see little of their children growing up.

The Horse child: Babies born in the year of the Horse make fiercely independent children and because they want to go their own way and do their own thing, it is very likely that they will leave home at quite a young age in order to forge their own lives. Of especial note with these young colts is that too many rules and too great a demand on conformity will make these youngsters defiant and rebellious. At school their quick minds learn readily. Communication skills and languages are perhaps their forte. The secret of keeping Horse children happy is in keeping them busy with plenty of hobbies and activities for their hungry and fertile little minds.

Health: The saying 'strong as a horse' just about sums up this group of people. Born with indomitable energy, Horses simply leave lesser mortals seemingly mooching about on the starting line.

Careers, hobbies and pastimes: Because of their charm and highly developed sense of diplomacy, Horse-born individuals make excellent tacticians, politicians and diplomats. At work, they score on all fronts where languages and communications are involved. Flexible working hours are far more suited to them than the strictly regimented nine-to-five system. Besides, with their ability to do three jobs at the same time, they're more likely to get their work done twice as quickly as their fellow employees. So, having accomplished their tasks, what's the point of hanging around and just twiddling their thumbs – they might as well go off and enjoy themselves. And once outside the office, sports of all types will attract Horse-born folk. Circuit training, running, athletics, any team games or contact sports will all suit. And so, of course, will horse riding.

THE SHEEP

Keynotes to Character: Sensitive, careful, prudent, pernickety, punctilious, neat, tidy.

The Sign: The Sheep is the sign of the Arts.

Personality:
Socially, domestically and politically, people belonging to the Sheep category are the least likely to make waves. They are quite happy with the status quo. Not in a hurry to question authority, they respect order and pay attention to rules and regulations that are laid down by laws and by society. Knowing their character, then, it is not surprising to find that the year of the Sheep is a time of peace.

And it is this desire for peace and for a tranquil life that leads those born under the Sheep influence to avoid conflict of any kind. Indeed, so great is their need for harmony that they tend to go along with the flow, contenting themselves with the majority consensus rather than putting forward their own point of view of standing up for their own rights. Many, then, consider Sheep-born individuals to be complacent, and even go so far as to accuse them of being sycophantish 'yes men'.

Moreover, what seems to lend weight to this argument is that Sheep folk have a strongly inherent herding instinct and function a good deal better when part of a group than when on their own. Consequently, because they so contentedly follow the rest of the pack, often quite unquestioningly so, another accusation that is levelled at this group is that its members seriously lack individuality. They are not, in any sense of the word, pushy types and, with a few exceptions, aren't particularly noted for making outstanding leaders. But they do make formidable diplomats, always seeking to find the compromise, the middle road, the peaceful solution that will satisfy everybody. Politically speaking, this is the sign of the moderate and the democrat and, unlike others who tend to stick their necks out, precisely by keeping their heads down, Sheep manage to withstand and survive the many vagaries of life.

Whether it is because Sheep are such nice and pleasant people, or whether it is because they are born under a lucky star, fortune seems to favour them. It is quite possible that because they are so mild, unassuming and whimsical, they would not be capable of making their fortune in life by their own efforts and endeavours. Yet many seem one way or another to attract success and money whether through legacies, patronage or popular acceptance via the mass media. Consequently, this popularity and success makes for an easy life where Sheep-folk are concerned.

If these people are in public life it would be wise for them to engage the services of reliable agents and managers who would protect and promote their interests, advise them on handling their money and encourage them to get the very best possible out of their talents.

Generally, subjects of this sign are careful in all they do, they are neat and tidy, appreciating an orderly environment in which to live and work. Often described as fastidious, they are not only the most gentle, but also likely to have the most gentility of all the animal signs. Certainly, there is nothing base or crude about them, indeed they possess excellent manners and the males particularly adhere to the old-fashioned gentlemanly code, behaving courteously and chivalrously at all times.

Yet there' is another side to these normally passive, sensitive and graceful creatures – they do like to show off. Switch on the spotlight and they simply can't help but turn into performers and showmen.

In Chinese tradition, this is the most feminine of all the twelve signs. Generally, those born in the year of the Sheep are attracted to the Arts and many are highly creative. But they are practical, too, so that for them Art must also be functional and, conversely, every-day functional objects must also reflect inherent beauty. Couple their talents to their manual dexterity and it is not difficult to see why so many Sheep-born people are gifted craftsmen and women.

Though many will gravitate towards a creative or artistic career, there will be just as many who are attracted to the vocational occupations. Sheep are kind, helpful, considerate and sympathetic people and so will be found in all fields of the caring professions – social workers, nurses, doctors, veterinary surgeons, and all manner of healers, practitioners and therapists in complementary medicine.

With their strong artistic inclinations, it is not surprising that Sheep-folk have a keen eye for beauty and they simply adore exquisite things. Just as psychologically they need peace and harmony, so physically they need to be surrounded by beauty both in their living and working environment. Without pleasant or conducive surroundings these people could so easily become depressed and dispirited.

Domestic in the extreme, people born during the year of the Sheep love their family and their homes. It is therefore essential to their peace of mind that they create around themselves a warm, harmonious and united domestic environment.

The Sheep lover: In matters of Love, it is the Sheep's heart which rules its head. These people work best as part of a team, so a secure, stable and loving relationship is essential for their emotional well-being. Perhaps more than any other sign, Sheep are home-lovers and are tailor-made for marriage and family life. Indeed the family is so important to them that when they do settle down, it is likely to be round the corner from mum and dad, or from their other married brothers and sisters, where they feel they are cushioned and have the full protection of the extended family to fall back on if needed. Next to love and security, they crave peace and harmony, consequently they will bend over backwards within their relationships to keep things running smoothly. As they hate discord of any kind their partners shouldn't ever expect them to get embroiled in an argument for these people, quite infuriatingly sometimes, will simply retreat into silence. As lovers they can be clingy and dependent. Highly sensual, they will adore physical contact and delight in kissing, cuddling and making love. However, despite all their need for tranquility, partners of Sheep should note that these people want what they want and will all too often wear down opposition with tears and tantrums in order to get their own way!

The Sheep parent: Parents born in the year of the Sheep possess a strong mothering instinct. Possessiveness is one of the negative attributes of this sign and many a Sheep mother and father must be mindful of a tendency to smother their offspring. But in general these are deeply affectionate people with an immense love of their families and their home. Good manners and the social graces are so important to Sheep-born folk that parents will instil them into their children from a very early age.

The Sheep child: Youngsters born under the influence of the Sheep are clingy, dependent and affectionate. They have a tendency to cry easily and when either upset or unable to get what they want they may well resort to sulkiness. Often lacking in self-confidence, they like to feel protected and secure and they need a great deal of support from their parents and teachers early in their lives. Generally speaking, these little lambs are polite and respectful towards their parents and superiors, neat and tidy in their habits, shun conflict and rebellion whenever and wherever possible and are, on the whole, extremely easy to get on with. The one proviso to remember with Sheep children is never to tease or make fun of them for their fragile sensitivities are deeply affected by embarrassment and ridicule.

Health: The need for love, security and emotional stability are at the root of the Sheep's well-being. Without these comforts, natives of this sign would soon find their unhappiness taking its toll on their health. Equally, the Sheep's sensitivity is responsible for any malaise they might suffer. However, they are blessed with staying power and if they can keep their personal relationships together, they will be able to maintain the peace and stability that is so essential to their good health.

Careers, hobbies and pastimes: Listening to music or playing an instrument make excellent pastimes for Sheep-born people. Games and activities that involve the whole family particularly appeal. When considering sports, team games (especially the non-contact sort) will be more suitable than solitary, individual games such as long-distance running. As far as careers are concerned, the caring or vocational professions attract this group. Anything to do with the Arts would be highly appropriate and the performing arts would come into this category too. Because of their tactful approach to people, the diplomatic service would benefit from the Sheep's skills as well as any other profession in which tact and diplomacy are of the essence.

THE MONKEY

Keynotes to Character: Mercurial, quick-witted, maverick, resourceful, resilient, impetuous, indiscreet.

The Sign: The Monkey is the sign of imagination.

Personality:
Cleverness, intelligence and quick-wits are the salient characteristics of the Monkey folk. They possess keen, Mercurial minds that allow them to size up any situation simply at a mere glance.

Ever ingenious and inventive, their natural cunning ensures they play their cards right in life. From a very early age they learn the intricacies of social skills – how to interact with best effect, how to get on with others, how to get around people, how to get precisely what they want from a relationship. These people with their poise, their control and their self-assurance have vast resources of inborn charm at their disposal which ensures them general popularity and also guarantees the fulfillment of their aims and ambitions in life.

Their inventiveness, however, suggests not only a skilful or dexterous mentality but also a tendency, when necessary, to bend the truth to their own advantage. Monkeys have a habit of making up their own reality as they go along. All too often the boundary between fantasy and reality can be rather smudged, fact merges with fiction and, in their scheme of things, truth and untruth often make easy bedfellows. And if their not quite so high standards of morality should outrage the rest of society, the Monkey's agile and nimble minds, coupled with their immense resourcefulness will, quick as lightning, manage somehow to twist the situation to their own advantage so as to completely vindicate themselves and save face.

People born under this influence have an innately low boredom threshold. Inquisitive in the extreme and forever believing that the grass is greener elewhere, they need to find continual stimulation to keep themselves interested and amused. They possess an impish sense of humour and what might be described almost as a talent for mischief-making which they use to liven things up around them. In the modern idiom, Monkey-folk can be right little stirrers.

However, some may exercise a rather Machiavellian streak for they are all too easily able to manipulate others. This is because Monkey types possess acute psychological perspicacity which enables them to read people like books, spotting a mile away their strengths, their weak points and their soft spots. In particular, women under the Monkey influence can play rather subtle games with members of the opposite sex, quietly seducing them with their feminine whiles.

But on the positive side, they are highly adaptable and versatile. They quickly assimilate facts and figures, picking up new skills and techniques in the twinkling of an eye. This is a tremendous asset for them not only in the workplace but socially as well for, in the ability to absorb the manners and mores around them and being able to automatically mimic the behaviour of those they are with, they can easily fit into whatever company, whatever social group they find themselves with. The saying 'when in Rome, do as the Romans' fits none of the other signs quite so comfortably as it does the Monkey personality.

With their agile mentality, problem solving is both their forte and their great joy. Highly intelligent, they are brilliant innovators, enjoying the challenge of pitting their wits against the odds. In business it is their opportunism coupled with their sang-froid and keen competitive instinct that gives them an eye for that gap in the market, that tiny opening in which only Monkeys can squeeze themselves. And once they have instilled themselves, no matter how tiny the crack, it is their ability to turn their hands to anything that will bring them ultimate success and, in many cases, even make their fortune.

Though the renowned adaptability of the Monkey personality takes those born under this sign into a variety of occupations, many will naturally gravitate towards show business. This is because Monkey-born people have a compelling need to be noticed, to leave a lingering impression, a memory of themselves behind wherever they go. But, because they are such audacious people, and because they care very little about their reputations, it does not matter much to them whether the impression they create is one of pleasure or of shock. It is simply a case of the more publicity they can generate around themselves, the happier they are.

The Monkey lover: Monkeys are clever, social, witty people and these are the very qualities they will look for in their relationships with others. And, being the gregarious sort, they normally have a wide circle of friends and acquaintances who provide them with the mental and social stimulation that is so important to the Monkey's well-being. But the natural curiosity and desire for new experiences that is such a mordant drive to those born in this year, means that all too often serious long-term relationships simply don't provide enough excitement to maintain their interest. These people revel in the thrill of the new, consequently short-term love affairs tend to suit this group best. Mischievous rascals, particularly through their earlier years, they delight in stirring things up, in upsetting the status quo, and then standing back to watch the sparks fly. So too in their relationships, and if there's the slightest hint of danger, of intrigue, of naughtiness or of downright outrageous behaviour attached, so much the better. In love, no other sign produces more charming, amusing and romantic companions than this one and once a Monkey does decide to settle down in a permanent relationship they will make a splendidly stimulating partner.

The Monkey parent: In general, people born in a Monkey year make interesting parents. Despite their inherent superficiality they are, nevertheless, committed to the task of parenthood and they take their responsibilities seriously. On the whole tolerant and open-minded they can, nevertheless, be quick to anger and then, just as quickly, regain their good humour. From their children's point of view, the best thing about Monkey parents is that they are such Peter Pan types, never truly growing up, so they can easily respond to their offspring on their own level. And, because Monkeys have such versatile temperaments and personalities, their diversity of interests will happily keep their children stimulated and amused.

The Monkey child: Insatiably curious about the world

around them, Monkey children find it easy to learn and to pick up new ideas. They are great fidgets both mentally and physically, unable to sit still or to stop their minds from ticking over for even one minute. Full of energy, full of good humour, full of high jinks, they especially love playing practical jokes on people. As befits their sign, these youngsters have a tendency to 'monkey around' and will be often found mimicking their elders and betters. Indeed they can be cheeky little monkeys, tiny tricksters even from a very young age, ingenious at discovering ways of getting around people and of getting what they want. They are notorious for lying through their teeth in order to save their skins but they do it so skilfully and with such charm that invariably one ends up giving them the benefit of the doubt.

Careers, hobbies and pastimes: Monkey-born people are salesmen par excellence. Whether it is that they are peddling their wares or simply selling themselves, they make brilliant wheeler-dealers, born with the gift of the gab and able to charm the hind leg off a donkey. So anything to do with sales, PR and advertising would suit this group. Journalism or other work with the press, acting and any sort of TV work attract the Monkey. In terms of hobbies and pastimes, word puzzles, computer games and team sports where agility is of the essence are typical Monkey-type activities.

Health: Monkeys are prone to depression. But, whatever might ail Monkey-folk, whether physical or psychological, they are quick to recover. Thanks to their indomitable spirits, they simply pick themselves up, dust themselves down and start all over again. Besides, there's far too much do to, far too many places to visit, far too much to see in life for the restless Monkeys to allow themselves to be ill for long.

THE ROOSTER

Keynotes to Character: Bright-eyed and bushy-tailed, showy, canny, extrovert, flamboyant, open.

The Sign: The Rooster is the sign of honesty.

Personality:
People born during a Rooster year are hard nuts to crack. Strong-minded, tough and resilient, they display all the pride and self-confidence in life that a cockerel does in a chicken run.

Rooster-born folk possess powerful personalities. Assertive and determined, they like to stand on their own two feet. And though this is a 'feminine' sign, people born under its influence are notoriously dominant, some would go as far as to say downright bossy, if not even thoroughly intimidating at times.

These people are born organisers. They are tidy-minded and like to keep everything neat and ship-shape.

In their homes there won't be a newspaper out of place; at work they are methodical and sticklers for detail. Their affairs will be all in order, accounts up to the minute and documents systematically filed away.

They function best and are most comfortable in an environment where everything is organised and their schedules programmed. In general, they are not the sort to rush their fences. When it comes to making decisions of any kind, Roosters prefer to weigh up the balance and carefully consider all sides of a situation before coming to a conclusion.

The same applies to relationships. Emotionally, Roosters are said to be passionate and though they may possess a very active sex-drive, they tend to lack firm personal commitment when it comes to serious relationships. Moreover, they can be rather shallow in their feelings towards others.

The management of finances is perhaps their forte both on a private and professional level. Flashy in most areas of their lives, when it comes to money Roosters are prudent and careful, excellent at husbandry, sometimes even paring down to the bone, skimping and scraping so that they can enjoy the pleasure of seeing their bank accounts grow fat. They are very much the sort of people who can make a pound stretch to a fiver. They are also brilliant managers of other people's money, recognising in an instant how to control funds and allocate budgets. Financial advisers, bank managers, accountants, money lenders would all do well to be born in the year of the Rooster.

These people have an abundance of energy and stamina both in their working lives and in their leisure pursuits. Often they take on far more than they can cope with and consequently don't always manage to come up with the promised goods. In the same vein they adore parties, outings and social gatherings, dancing until the early hours of the morning, burning the candle at both ends.

Distinctly achievement-motivated, Roosters have a compulsion for winning. They need to feel they are the best, the cleverest, the wittiest, the ones who stand out in a crowd. And the are not happy unless they can gain the advantage over another person, get the better of whoever they are with. The chap who isn't happy unless he simply has the very last word on the matter simply has to be born under the influence of this sign.

Selfishness and a sense of grandeur, of self-importance, are perhaps the most negative of the Rooster qualities. They can be conceited creatures, bragging about their abilities and accomplishments, praising their own self-worth and expecting just as much praise back from others too. And it is this conceit that makes them vain and boastful, that gives them a strong egotistical need to constantly be the centre of attention.

And yet it is this very quality that makes them such amusing companions. Excellent at small talk they can, with their idle banter, be the life and soul of any party, entertaining all those around with their sparkling repartee and fascinating little anecdotes.

Indeed, they are talkative types, outspoken, frank, open, honest – but a little too blunt at times, perhaps even abrasive might well describe their manner. This is due in part to a rather critical streak in their natures and, coupled with a tendency to tactlessness and intolerance, it is easy to see how Roosters have earned a reputation for bitchiness and sarcasm.

There is an interesting dichotomy about the Rooster personality. On the one hand they are conservative and traditionalist in their outlook. On the other, they are dramatic and theatrical. The fine colourful plumage of the farmyard bird suggests that those born under the influence of the Rooster have a tendency to extravagant dress. They especially love showy clothes and uniforms with lots of gold braiding. And when gorgeously attired in all their finery, they will be seen to strut about, displaying their fine feathers for all the world to see and admire.

The Rooster lover: Emotionally, Roosters see the world as either black or white – with hardly any shades of grey in between. Consequently, when it comes to individual people, Roosters will immediately either love them or hate them on sight. The salient characteristic attributed to these people is their honesty and Roosters are never backwards in coming forwards to speak their mind. It is rather helpful to the success of their relationships, then, if their partners could develop a thick skin – and fast – because Roosters are notoriously critical people and equally notoriously blunt. Their sheer lack of tact, coupled with a rather sanctimonious holier-than-thou attitude to life, has been responsible for the breaking up of many a Rooster's marriage. Yet Rooster males are dashing, handsome chaps and will have young women flocking to be at their sides. Their Hen counterparts, stylish in the classical vein, will attract their suitors through their no-nonsense, down-to-earth approach to life. In love, neither male nor female Rooster will wear their hearts on their sleeves; indeed these are rather dark horses who keep even the minutest detail about their sexual exploits or their love affairs strictly to themselves. And because of their scrupulous honesty, when happily settled in a permanent relationship, Roosters are highly unlikely to deceive or cheat on their partners.

The Rooster parent: Rooster parents can be strict, conformist and rather old-fashioned. Perhaps not the most sensitive mothers and fathers of the animal zodiac, nor indeed the most compassionate towards their offspring, they are sticklers for detail and strong on discipline. Staunch believers in the status quo, many a Rooster father will be heard to preface his admonishments to his youngsters with, 'When I was a boy we were expected to . . .'

The Rooster child: In general, childhood for Roosters is a happy and contented time although there may be one or two slight hiccoughs to overcome. Youngsters belonging to this sign are bright and vivacious with a cheeky sort of charm. All Roosters love dressing up and little fledglings in particular will amuse themselves happily for hours if given a bag of old clothes, a few hats and some broken baubles from the jewellery box. At school, though they are attentive, hard-working and keen to learn, they are perhaps not the most academic high-fliers one is likely to meet. However, they will excel in all the subjects where social skills are required and many a young Rooster will distinguish themselves on the sports field.

Careers, hobbies and pastimes: Publishing, journalism, the performing arts, amateur dramatics, are all favoured under this sign. But banking and anything to do with the world of finance are especially suited to the Rooster mentality. Gardening is a particular passion and joy, and so is everything connected with agriculture, horticulture and perhaps in certain cases, landscaping. Sports are greatly enjoyed and many a Rooster will be a professional in this field. And, because of their fiercely personal competitiveness, they are much more inclined to go in for the one-to-one type of activity rather than team games – tennis, golf, boxing, etc. – where each Rooster is able to shine individually and has the opportunity to outsmart their opponent. And then of course the Rooster can go forward to receive the champion's crown of laurels which, after all, is only theirs by right anyway, isn't it?

Health: Because Roosters are so active and energetic and enjoy taking part in sports, they do tend to keep themselves fairly fit. Psychologically, those born under this influence are inclined to dramatic mood swings and should learn to keep on a more even keel. Moreover, their high standards of excellence coupled with their competitiveness puts them in the Category A grouping for stress and tension with all the accompanying health problems these conditions produce.

THE DOG

Keynotes to Character: Amicable, dependable, loyal, dedicated, devoted, candid, open and frank.

The Sign: The Dog is the sign of fidelity.

Personality:
Amongst the animal zodiac, Dog individuals are the most humanitarian. These are the givers in life, prepared to sacrifice their own dreams, ambitions and desires for the sake of others, and particularly so, for those they love. Born to serve, they are the carers, unselfishly putting the needs of others first and themselves last.

Fiercely loyal to those they love, Dogs are ever ready to jump to the defence of any member of their family or friends who is being attacked by either word or deed. Such selfless, humanitarian instincts suggests a penchant for championing the underdog and indeed these people, for whom equal rights, civil liberties and justice are of paramount importance, are renowned for taking up the cudgels on behalf of the lesser able.

Sometimes, however, their willingness to help can be misinterpreted and they may be seen as nosey-parkers, meddling in other people's affairs and all too ready to give advice where perhaps advice has not been sought. Equally, because they genuinely feel they know best, they can sometimes appear bossy, walking in, barking orders and taking charge of the whole situation.

But it is a strong idealistic streak in their natures that makes them genuinely well-meaning people and indeed many turn their talents to vocational or community work. Those Dogs for whom justice, fair-play and social reforms are especially of major concern will work selflessly and tirelessly to right injustice and inequality and to improve the general lot of the less fortunate in society.

Dog people are solid, steady workers who put consistent effort into whatever they are doing. Indeed, they are persistent types, certainly not given to letting up once they have set their minds on an objective – a characteristic which some might describe as obstinacy or even downright bloody-mindedness. But, thoroughly sensible and aware of their physical and mental limitations, they pace themselves to the requirement of their tasks and don't take on more than they can reasonably handle.

With their forthright honesty and true moral integrity they soon become pillars of society, respected for their views and trusted by all who come to know them. Staunchly loyal to both friends and superiors, they will always make time to listen to other people's problems and to give comfort whenever they can. The saying 'a man's best friend is his dog' just about sums up these true, dependable and faithful people who always seem to have a kind word to say about everyone.

One problem associated with some members of this

sign is that they find it difficult to adapt to change and many prefer to stick it out in the same situation, no matter how unpleasant, rather than face the unknown and start all over again. Perhaps this is because Dogs are innately pessimistic and inclined to expect the worst to happen. And it is this tendency to see the negative side of things that can all too often mar their enjoyment of life and can even spoil the happiness they might otherwise be deriving from their intimate relationships. But when absolutely forced to make changes they will, although very reluctantly so. To compound the misery they feel because of their lack of enthusiasm for their new situation and circumstances, they tend to become wistful and nostalgic about the past.

Another problem that people born under the Dog influence may experience is an inherent inner anxiety. Though seemingly composed on the surface, they possess a feeling of uneasiness deep down inside that tends to make them worry and fret, very often needlessly. And yet they are strongly intuitive. But this, at times, probably only serves to make matters worse because, like all good bloodhounds, they seem to scent when danger is about and all too easily they can become suspicious of people they don't know and of situations with which they are unfamiliar.

Of all the animals in the Chinese Zodiac, Dogs are the least materialistic for they are unselfish individuals who care more about people than they do about money or success.

The Dog lover: Though Dogs are often described as slow to make friends – they don't easily entrust their affections – when they do, those friendships are for life. In fact, personal relationships for the Dog-born are THE most essential and most important components of their lives: money, power, success, all the elements that might motivate members of other signs, simply don't mean a thing to Dogs without first and foremost a loving partner by their side and a stable and secure family and home life. Some born under this influence, though, may encounter difficulties in finding a life-long mate principally because of the importance they attach to their relationships, but also because of their anxieties and their mistrust of people they don't know. Consequently, they could miss many an opportunity to develop an intimate rapport with suitors who could potentially develop into otherwise most worthy partners. In love, the most salient characteristic of Dogs is their loyalty. Once these people have pledged their allegiance, or sworn their marriage vows, they will stick to their partners through thick and thin. Few more constant, more faithful companions will be found than those born under the influence of the Dog.

The Dog parent: Children of a Dog mother or father are fortunate indeed for in them they will have inherited not so much a parent but more a friend. Dog parents are truly perceptive and aware when it comes to their offspring, allowing them to develop at their own pace and to find their own niche in society. They are caring and supportive, always ready to hear them out, to lend a shoulder for them to cry on, to provide a sounding board for their ideas and aspirations, a word of comfort when required. Neither possessive nor restrictive, these parents carry their beliefs of freedom and equal rights into the very heart of their homes so that their children are allowed free expression and the freedom to be themselves.

The Dog child: Like all young puppies, Dog youngsters are cute and lovable. They are blessed with a warm and cuddly nature, friendly, easy-going and well-adjusted. They love their family and home and are quite happy to potter around their own familiar territory. From a very young age Dog children develop a certain presence, a bearing akin to self-esteem that makes them stand out and makes others respect them. Full of common-sense, they can be relied upon to get their work done without too much hassle and will always be at hand to offer their assistance when help is required, or when younger brothers or sisters need the benefit of their protection. Mentally these little puppy Dogs are alert and observant, eager to learn and just as eager to please.

Careers, hobbies and pastimes: With their intuitive powers and insight into human nature, Dogs make excellent psychologists, counsellors, nurses, doctors, vets and general carers of the old and the sick. With their objectivity they would equally make good solicitors, lawyers and general advisers. And with their humanitarian ideals, respected political or religious figures. But, best of all, they make wonderful friends. Dogs are energetic and full of vitality and so enjoy a good deal of sport and physical activity. Being gregarious, they also like the company of others, so team sports will be ideal. Friendships are important to Dogs so they will greatly enjoy social gatherings of all descriptions. In their spare time they derive great pleasure from all sorts of handicraft projects, gardening and D.I.Y.

Health: Some Dog people, depending at what time of day and when in the year they were born, can be fairly highly-strung. Most, however, are sturdy types who can, when necessary, withstand a good deal of mental and physical hardship with philosophical acceptance. However, for those who suffer from anxiety, ways and means should be sought to combat that deeply-felt uneasiness and thus put their minds to rest.

THE PIG

Keynotes to Character: Domestic, hard-working, down-to-earth, unassuming, happy with his or her lot.

The Sign: The Pig is the sign of honesty.

Personality:

People born in the year of the Pig have a taste for la dolce vita. Possessing a strong sense of luxury, they can be extravagant and take great pleasure in pampering themselves and their loved ones. Fond of buying little treats for themselves or presents they know will please others, they delight in the stimulation of the senses. Not for them the endless rush of busy-ness and activity because for Pigs, it is a life of ease and of pleasure that is so very conducive to their complacent nature.

But, when they do need to work they will roll up their sleeves and get stuck in. At these times a half-hearted attitude simply won't do: where they're concerned it's all or nothing. So Pigs will work hard when needs must,

77

but then they compensate for their efforts by rewarding themselves with little luxuries, holiday trips or simply indulging in their favourite leisure pursuits.

But at the same time, Pig folk can be very practical, logical and down-to-earth. They may at times be considered somewhat cool and reserved because, blessed as they are with plenty of composure and self-control, they don't usually allow emotion to cloud the issue.

Cheerful, generally contented with their lot, Pigs love company and social life. They adore having fun and, with their light-hearted, frothy attitude to life, they make amusing folk to be with. Being gregarious creatures, people are important to them and it is unusual to find solitary Pigs. Furthermore, those born under this sign find it very easy to make friends and also seem to hang on to them for life.

Pigs are described as uncomplicated souls, unpretentious, down-to-earth and lacking in dissimulation, – although sometimes they find it necessary to prevaricate, but then only ever so slightly.

Tactlessness is perhaps their worst characteristic – some tend not only to put their foot in it but could veritably fit a whole shoe store in their mouths! But although they are not renowned for their diplomacy, Pigs are excellent at pouring oil on turbulent seas so are invaluable to have around in peace-making or gap-bridging situations.

Some Pigs, it is true to say, lack self-reflection and insight. They are certainly no way near as perspicacious as, say, the Monkey. But then they more than make up for this with their big-heartedness and generosity – something which unfortunately is all too often taken advantage of and Pigs are all too easily taken for a ride.

Though generally tolerant and fairly placid people, when absolutely backed into a corner, make no mistake about it, Pigs can turn vicious. When they find that their friendship and good nature have been seriously abused, they will give no quarter and that friendship will somewhat unceremoniously be cut short.

Home is a passion where Pig folk are concerned and many will put a great deal of effort into their domestic environment, decorating it stylishly, adding their own creative touches, so typical of the Pig's talents for handicrafts and domestic skills. And of all the solid, home-oriented virtues, it is in the culinary arts that Pigs excel. Indeed, it is probably fair to say that of the signs of the Chinese Horoscope, Pigs make the best cooks of all.

When it comes to entertaining, these people refuse to cut corners. Extravagant, excessive and sensually indulgent, when they invite their friends round for a bite, you can be sure it won't be a bit of bread and cheese they'll be presented with, but a truly magnificent feast laid out on the table complete with sparkling crystal and groaning with the family silver!

Yes, Pigs certainly know how to put on the ritz in style and, just as much as they love food and parties and friends and having a thoroughly good time, so they adore dressing up. Ladies of the sign in particular will dress to the hilt – sometimes though with a danger of being just a little too ostentatious.

Perhaps they can be accused of showing off, of exhibitionism, of being flirtatious, even licentious at times, but there is no doubt that Pigs in general are very good sorts: honest, decent, generous, supportive, loyal to their friends and thoroughly trustworthy.

The Pig lover: Above all else Pigs are sensual, self-indulgent creatures. They adore anything that smacks of physical pleasure whether it is gorging themselves with sweetmeats or idling a whole day away with their new-found heart-throbs between their satin sheets. And, needless to say, their vast self-indulgent appetites include the pleasures of sexual intercourse. Passionate by nature, some younger Pigs could tend towards promiscuity whilst some of the older ones, unable to control their sexual desires, could well become bawdy and lascivious. Unfortunately for them, 'grande passion' seems somehow to befog many a Pig and when deeply smitten they have a habit of going all silly, their emotions becoming rather transparent and at that point they can become putty in the hands of more unscrupulous types who can induce them to behave quite out of character. In the main, though, Pigs are loving and loyal to their mates, caring and considerate towards those they love. And in any close, intimate relationship it is friendship that the Pig lover will value most. Settled with the right partner, these generous, warm-hearted individuals will enjoy happy and contented lives, developing their talents within that supportive framework and devoting themselves completely to their family and their loved ones.

The Pig parent: Pig mothers and fathers take a fairly cool and level-headed approach to child-rearing. Because they are generally fun-loving people, they will enjoy their children but will, nevertheless, ensure that their youngsters grow up good-mannered and well-educated. Extravagant themselves, they have a tendency to spoil their children and, because they derive enormous pleasure from dispensing happiness, they are unlikely to deny their offspring anything they desire. Pigs are domestic creatures at heart so their homes and their families are very important to them. As parents they will give their children an easy time and provide a fairly relaxed and easy-going atmosphere in which to grow and develop. With their laid-back attitude to life, Pigs create a calming influence upon which to build their parent-child relationship with their offspring.

The Pig child: Children born in the year of the Pig

make stable, well-balanced, uncomplicated and happy-go-lucky little individuals. Warm and affectionate, they are cuddly types, popular both at home and amongst their friends. At school, little piglets are self-confident, industrious and obedient, getting on with their school work when told to. Though many won't particularly excel academically they are, nevertheless, quick learners. Honest as the live-long day, they cannot tell a lie – principally because if they try to, their guilt can be seen a mile away! Being slightly on the complacent side, they work best in a structured, organized environment where their skills and talents can be harnessed and directed. With lots of support and plenty of food to satisfy their huge appetite, these children will breeze through their early years giving very little trouble at all. Strong little mites, they can put up with a great deal of physical discomfort without complaining. Moreover, their cheerful disposition and general bonhomie make these little individuals a pleasure to have around.

Careers, hobbies and pastimes: Entertaining, partying, social functions and all types of leisure activities are especially associated with those born during the year of the Pig. Mixing with people, enjoying themselves and generally having fun are the prerequisites for keeping them happy and healthy. Because they like to pamper themselves, massage, reflexology and aromatherapy would make them feel really spoilt. And considering their large appetites, a spell or two at a health farm would do them some good now and again. As far as sports are concerned, the 'cleaner', more glamorous activities suit this group best: tennis, golf, ski-ing, cricket, horse-riding. Handicrafts and artistic or creative occupations are tailor-made for Pig people. The beauty industry, fashion, design, journalism, publishing, theatre and television would all attract.

Health: Generally speaking, Pigs are robust, hale and

hearty types. They can put up with a good deal of physical discomfort without making any fuss for they possess quite a high pain threshold. Their weakness in life, however, is eating and drinking so for the sake of their health (let alone their figures!), they should watch their appetites and practise some self-control. Exercise, too, is essential for their overall well-being.

Chapter 3

PREDICTING THE FUTURE

Trends in the next cycle

The Chinese Horoscope is not only a means of character assessment, but it can also be used to give us glimpses into the future. Just as a wine vintage produces subtle changes from year to year according to weather conditions, rainfall, atmospheric pressure, the degeneration of the soil, etcetera, so each year, according to Chinese astrologers, has a distinctive 'flavour' which distinguishes it from its predecessor and which is strongly influenced by the nature of the symbolical creature that is its figure-head.

Years run sequentially from Rat to Pig in their 12-year cycle and thus by understanding the character of each symbol it is possible to gauge the salient characteristics that will colour each period of time. And just as people born under the influence of any one of the twelve signs will respond differently to any of the other eleven, whether compatible, hostile or indifferent, so it is possible to assess how these individuals as a whole will react within any particular year.

Listed below, then, are the highlights associated with the next 12 years, showing the nature and trends that might be expected for each year. In addition, hints on additional prospects and reactions are given which, of course, are necessarily generalised but which, it is hoped, will provide a little advanced warning so that evasive action may be taken, if required, or opportunities not allowed to slip through the net.

1994 THE YEAR OF THE DOG

Following the self-centred stance of the preceding year, this one turns its sights firmly back onto the family and home. All matters concerning protection and security, whether domestically, financially or politically will take precedence this year. The Dog symbolises idealism so humanitarian causes, questions of personal liberty, human rights, justice and freedom of speech will become salient now. It is a year in which integrity, moral values and high principles will outweigh material considerations. This is also a highly favourable time in which to marry.

Auspicious year for: Tigers, Rabbits, Horses, Monkeys, Dogs, Pigs
Difficult year for: Dragons, Sheep
Beware finances: Snakes
Beware relationships: Rats, Oxen, Roosters

1995 THE YEAR OF THE PIG

This is a year for tying up loose ends, for finalising deals and putting the finishing touches to all those projects that have been lying about unfinished. As the Pig closes the 12-year cycle, it is not an auspicious year for starting anything new but it is a time for reaping benefits from past efforts. It is a rather laisser-faire time, a period of relaxation, of pleasure and self-indulgence. Family ties, relationships, social life and entertainment will be to the fore with extravagance and impulsive spending going through the roof. In all, a time of peace, a time of rest and a time of good-will all round.

Auspicious year for: Oxen, Dragons, Sheep, Roosters, Dogs, Pigs
Difficult year for: Rabbits, Snakes, Monkeys
Beware finances: Rats, Horses
Beware relationships: Tigers

1996 THE YEAR OF THE RAT

As the 12-year cycle opens with the Year of the Rat this, then, is the year for new beginnings, a time when fresh opportunities will present themselves. It is a year for laying down plans, for formulating new intiatives, starting new projects and generally turning over a new leaf. Radical changes, whether political, social, professional or domestic, may be instituted now with the confidence of development and success in subsequent years. Financial affairs are also heavily marked; well-thought out investments should flourish although precipitate gambling and wild speculation should be avoided. In general, a time for looking forwards and planning for the future.

Auspicious year for: Rats, Dragons, Snakes, Sheep, Monkeys
Difficult year for: Rabbits, Horses, Roosters, Pigs
Beware finances: Tigers
Beware relationships: Oxen

1997 THE YEAR OF THE OX

This year is characterised by responsibility and hard work. Those who are prepared to keep their heads down and put their shoulders to the wheel will no doubt reap just rewards. It is, however, a year that promises stability and all projects initiated in the preceding year should show a steady increase and slow but sure fruition. Agriculture and all to do with the land are especially starred now. In particular, this is a year for promoting family unity and strengthening family ties.

Auspicious year for: Rats, Oxen, Rabbits, Snakes, Roosters, Pigs
Difficult year for: Tigers, Dragons
Beware finances: Sheep, Dogs
Beware relationships: Horses, Monkeys

1998 THE YEAR OF THE TIGER

A dramatic year, often described as making its presence felt by all and sundry. Tension, upheaval and disasters of all kinds characterise this year. Unusual weather conditions, disruptions to communications and international crises may be expected. This is a year for daring deeds – but only for those favoured by the Tiger – the rest are advised to keep their heads down. It is considered unlucky to marry in the year of the Tiger for at this time relationships may be electrified, sparked, fizzled and then die out again. In general a vibrant and exciting time that will quicken the pulse, that will bring great progress and success to some but perhaps disaster to others.

Auspicious year for: Rats, Tigers, Rabbits, Dogs
Difficult year for: Oxen, Snakes, Monkeys
Beware finances: Horses, Roosters
Beware relationships: Dragons, Sheep, Pigs

1999 THE YEAR OF THE RABBIT

After the adrenalin surge of the past 12 months, the Year of the Rabbit is one of recuperation and comes as balm to soothe our wounds. This is essentially a time of peace and reconciliation, a time when the pace of life slows down, when social activities and leisure pursuits are given prominence. It is a long sabbatical: a year in which we can bask in the sun, put our feet up, pamper ourselves and generally take things easy.

Auspicious year for: Oxen, Tigers, Rabbits, Dragons, Sheep, Monkeys, Dogs, Pigs
Difficult year for: Horses
Beware finances: Roosters
Beware relationships: Rats, Dragons

2000 THE YEAR OF THE DRAGON

Significant events on a world-wide basis mark the beginning and ending of a Dragon year. This is a daring, flamboyant time, a year that brings with it a frisson of excitement, the thrill of danger, of the unexpected. Expansive gestures, ambitious schemes and lavish productions are the order of the day. But though feelings will be buoyed up by success and prosperity, the inadvertent may also experience dramatic disasters. In the Year of the Dragon, the Arts are particularly favourably aspected and good auguries are in store for those who marry, start a family or take on new commercial enterprises.

Auspicious year for: Rats, Tigers, Dragons, Monkeys, Roosters, Pigs
Difficult year for: Oxen, Snakes, Sheep
Beware finances: Dogs
Beware relationships: Rabbits, Horses

2001 THE YEAR OF THE SNAKE

This is a year for taking stock. It would do well to remember that still waters run deep and that although the surface may appear calm, there may be dangerous undercurrents below. In general, it is a time in which trickery, fraud, underhanded deeds, political chicanery, both on a national and international level, may be expected. It is a year for the confidence trickster and the con-man so caution should be the byword. For some it will be a year of sudden changes, of reversals and even disaster. The Arts, music, fashion, industry and business are all well-aspected now.

Auspicious year for: Oxen, Rabbits, Dragons, Snakes, Sheep, Roosters, Dogs
Difficult year for: Monkeys
Beware finances: Rats
Beware relationships: Tigers, Horses, Pigs

2002 THE YEAR OF THE HORSE

This is an erratic year characteristic of the volatile Horse. Typically, the pace will be brisk and action and energy will be the keywords of the moment. Those who demur will lose out. Businesses should prosper – but good accounting must be maintained otherwise the vagaries of the Horse may see many a commercial venture go to the wall. Similarly for domestic management where husbandry must be practised. Otherwise, a commercially buoyant year with a fast tempo where optimism and impulsive action set the tone.

Auspicious year for:	Tigers, Dragons, Horses, Sheep, Monkeys, Dogs, Pigs
Difficult year for:	Oxen, Snakes
Beware finances:	Rats
Beware relationships:	Rabbits, Roosters

2003 THE YEAR OF THE SHEEP

A quiet, tranquil year with peace and harmony being the order of the day. This is a year of reconciliation, of finding compromises and settling differences. It is not an auspicious time for pioneering ventures or for striking out on new projects. But it is one for consolidation, for practising husbandry, for thinking along humanitarian lines. Politically, this is a time for diplomacy, for the ratification of treaties and for forging international diplomatic relations. A prosperous time for the fashion industry, for love and marriage, for complementary medicine, and for the Arts and all creative endeavours.

Auspicious year for:	Rats, Rabbits, Snakes, Horses, Sheep, Roosters, Pigs
Difficult year for:	Tigers, Dogs
Beware finances:	Oxen, Dragons
Beware relationships:	Monkeys

2004 THE YEAR OF THE MONKEY

Although a lively, optimistic and progressive year where finances should see an upturn, there will be a decided undercurrent of insecurity. Gremlins and high jinks abound, so nothing this year should be taken for granted, whether politically, financially, professionally, domestically or emotionally! It is a year where agile, inventive minds, sheer guts and bravado will win out – those who can stomach the roller-coaster, outsmart the confidence-trickster, and bluff their way through, will come out unscathed. Those who can't withstand the japes will come unstuck. A particularly auspicious time for new inventions.

Auspicious year for: Rats, Oxen, Dragons, Horses, Monkeys, Roosters, Dogs
Difficult year for: Tigers, Snakes, Pigs
Beware finances: Rabbits
Beware relationships: Sheep

2005 THE YEAR OF THE ROOSTER

This is a year for looking outwards and upwards, a time to turn one's sights away from the domestic situation and towards the big world outside. The general emphasis is centred on the individual this year: image projection, career matters, management of personal affairs, aspiring to one's ambitions. Politically there will be a lot of strutting and gassing but it will all turn out to be hot air. On the whole, it will be an optimistic year where the independent will score perhaps at the expense of those who tend to be dependent on others and on society at large. It will also bring out the more selfish, superficial side of human nature, a desire to feather one's own nest, to have one's own voice heard above the rest. In all, an auspicious year for conspicuous consumption and especially for the catering trade.

Auspicious year for: Oxen, Tigers, Dragons, Snakes, Sheep, Roosters
Difficult year for: Rabbits, Horses, Dogs
Beware finances: Rabbits
Beware relationships: Sheep

Chapter 4

FAMOUS PEOPLE WHO SHARE YOUR SIGN

THE RAT

Marlon Brando
Doris Day
HM Queen Elizabeth the
    Queen Mother
HRH Prince Harry
HRH The Prince of Wales
HRH The Duke of York

Glenda Jackson
Gary Lineker
Lulu
Wayne Sleep
Yves St. Laurent
Andrew Lloyd Webber

THE OX

Jane Fonda
Gerald Ford
Dustin Hoffman
HRH Viscount Linley
HRH The Princess of Wales
Richard Nixon

Robert Redford
Vanessa Redgrave
Margaret Thatcher
Twiggy
Fatima Whitbread

THE TIGER

David Attenborough
Richard Branson
Valéry Giscard D'Estaing
Alec Guinness
Her Majesty The Queen
HRH The Princess Royal
Rudolf Nureyev

David Owen
Diana Rigg
David Steel
Pamela Stephenson
Terry Wogan
Stevie Wonder

THE RABBIT

Fidel Castro
John Cleese
David Frost
James Galway
Bob Geldof

Ali McGraw
Henry Miller
Griff Rhys-Jones
Selina Scott
Orson Welles

THE DRAGON

Jeffrey Archer
Geoff Boycott
Jimmy Connors
Kirk Douglas
Edward Heath
HRH Princess Beatrice
HRH Prince Edward

Lady Sarah
    Armstrong-Jones
Bonnie Langford
Yehudi Menuhin
Zandra Rhodes
Cliff Richard
Mel Smith
Ringo Starr

THE SNAKE

Ronnie Barker
Ernest Borgnine
Joe Brown
Glynn Christian
Tom Conti
Stefan Edberg

Hannah Gordon
David Hasselhoff
Nigel Hawthorne
Jacqueline Onassis
André Previn
Victoria Wood

THE HORSE

Neil Armstrong
Zola Budd
Clint Eastwood
Chris Evert
Samantha Fox
Billy Graham

HRH Princess Margaret
HRH Prince Michael of
    Kent
Neil Kinnock
Paul McCartney
Barbra Streisand
Raquel Welch

THE SHEEP

Muhammad Ali
Boris Becker
Ian Botham
Terence Conran
Catherine Deneuve
John Denver

Anna Ford
Mikhail Gorbachev
Mick Jagger
Billie-Jean King
James Michener

THE MONKEY

Sebastian Coe
Shirley Conran
Stephen Hendry
HRH Princess Michael of
  Kent
Walter Matthau

Pope John Paul II
Tim Rice
Angela Rippon
Diana Ross
Liz Taylor

THE ROOSTER

Dirk Bogarde
Michael Caine
Steve Davis
Steffi Graff
Michael Heseltine
Katharine Hepburn
HRH The Duchess of Kent

HRH Prince Philip
Deborah Kerr
Yoko Ono
Nancy Reagan
Peter Ustinov
Mary Quant

THE DOG

Brigitte Bardot
Charles Bronson
Carol Burnett
Cher
Zsa Zsa Gabor
Michael Jackson
HRH Prince William
Sophia Loren

Madonna
Liza Minelli
Ralph Nader
Ilie Nastase
Sylvester Stallone
Mother Teresa
Daley Thompson
Mary Whitehouse

THE PIG

Woody Allen
Julie Andrews
Brian Clough
Robin Day
Ben Elton
HRH The Duke of Kent

HRH The Duchess of York
Elton John
Henry Kissinger
John McEnroe
Ronald Reagan
Tracey Ullman